EDGE BOOKS™

THE WORLD'S TOP TENS

THE WORLD'S MOST NOTORIOUS Crooks

by Matt Doeden

Consultant:
Allan May
Contributing Writer
AmericanMafia.com

Capstone press®

Mankato, Minnesota

J
364.1092z
Doedn

Edge Books are published by Capstone Press,
151 Good Counsel Drive, P.O. Box 669, Mankato, Minnesota 56002.
www.capstonepress.com

Library of Congress Cataloging-in-Publication Data
Doeden, Matt.
    The world's most notorious crooks / by Matt Doeden.
    p. cm.—(Edge Books. The world's top tens)
    Summary: "Describes 10 of the world's most notorious crooks in a
countdown format"—Provided by publisher.
    Includes bibliographical references and index.
    ISBN-13: 978-0-7368-6440-4 (hardcover)
    ISBN-10: 0-7368-6440-7 (hardcover)
    1. Criminals—Biography. 2. Brigands and robbers—Biography. 3. Swindlers and
swindling—Biography. 4. Outlaws—Biography. I. Title. II. Series: Edge Books, the
world's top tens.
HV6245.D64 2007
364.1092'2—dc22   2006003284

Editorial Credits
Angie Kaelberer, editor; Kate Opseth, set designer; PhaseOne, book designer;
    Wanda Winch, photo researcher; Scott Thoms, photo editor

Photo Credits
Corbis/Bettmann, cover, 6, 12, 26 (top left); Jonathan Blair, 13, 26 (bottom right);
    Reuters/Joyce George, 24, 27 (bottom right); Underwood & Underwood, 22, 27
    (bottom left)
Courtesy of the Arizona Historical Society, Tucson. AHS# 28916, 4
Getty Images Inc./American Stock, 20, 27 (middle right); Hulton Archive, 16, 18, 27
    (top right, middle left); ImageDirect/Kevin Winter, 10, 26 (bottom left);
    Keystone, 9; MPI, 14, 27 (top left); Stone+/Michael Kelley, 29; Time-Life
    Pictures/Allan Grant, 8, 26 (top right)

1 2 3 4 5 6 11 10 09 08 07 06

TABLE OF

CONTENTS

In 1899, Pearl Hart was the first woman sent to Yuma Territorial Prison in Arizona. But she wasn't notorious enough to make our top 10 list.

Outlaws, gangsters, con artists, and thieves—their stories of bold crimes and daring escapes are fascinating. Even ruthless killers can turn into legends if their stories are exciting enough.

But what's the truth behind the crimes? Why do some people leave an honest life for a life on the run?

In the following pages, we'll look at the lives and crimes of some of the most famous and clever criminals in history. We'll see their careful plans, narrow escapes, and eventual downfalls. You won't find stories of serial killers or cannibals—the criminally insane don't have a place on this list. What you will find are the stories behind 10 of the world's most famous and fascinating criminals.

10

Victor Lustig was famous for his fake sale of the Eiffel Tower in Paris.

BORN:	Around 1890 in Czechoslovakia
OTHER SCHEMES:	Sold machines that made fake money
FYI:	Death certificate listed his occupation as "salesman"

Victor Lustig

Victor Lustig may have been the greatest con artist ever. After all, nobody else can claim to have sold the Eiffel Tower—twice!

No one is sure of his real name, but he usually called himself Count Victor Lustig. He pulled off many cons in his life, but his 1925 "sale" of the Eiffel Tower in Paris, France, put him above other con artists.

Lustig pretended to be a government official when he met with a group of men who were in the scrap metal business. Lustig told the men that the famous landmark was to be torn down and sold for its metal. After he left town with one Paris businessman's money, he came back and did it again. This time, though, the buyer went to the police. Lustig was forced to flee France.

Lustig moved to the United States, where he made counterfeit money. In 1935, he was sent to jail for passing $134 million in fake bills. He escaped by climbing from a window using a rope made of bed sheets. Lustig was caught a few weeks later. He died in prison in 1947.

9

Sutton (center) stood trial in 1952 in New York City.

BORN:	June 30, 1901, in Brooklyn, New York
NICKNAMES:	Slick Willie; Willie the Actor
QUOTE:	When asked why he robbed banks, Sutton said, "Because that's where the money is."

WILLIE Sutton

In 1950, Sutton was charged with robbing a New York City bank of about $60,000.

Willie Sutton was a master of disguise. His charm and wit made him one of the smoothest robbers of all time.

Sutton always carried a gun on his heists, but he never used it. He relied instead on disguises and his intelligence. He dressed as a postal worker, a police officer, a messenger, and a maintenance worker to gain entrance to banks and stores.

Sutton was also a master of prison escapes. Once, he and other inmates dressed as prison guards. The disguises fooled prison officials, even when the inmates carried ladders to the prison wall.

Sutton was released from prison in 1969. He then left his life of crime and worked for banks. Oddly enough, he helped them with security!

8

Today, Abagnale works with bank managers and police officers, instead of against them.

BORN:	April 27, 1948, in Bronxville, New York
NICKNAME:	The Skywayman
FYI:	Played by Leonardo DiCaprio in the 2002 movie *Catch Me if You Can*

FRANK ABAGNALE

Frank Abagnale Jr. was a smart kid. Probably too smart. At age 16, Abagnale ran away from home. He looked older than he was and easily passed for an adult. But as a high school dropout, he could get only low-paying jobs. He started writing checks for cash at stores and hotels. The problem was he didn't have any money in his account. He knew he had to keep moving to avoid getting caught.

When he was 18, Abagnale decided to pose as an airline pilot. He managed to get an airline uniform and used fake ID cards to get free travel around the world. But that wasn't his only scam. He made fake documents to get jobs as a doctor, lawyer, and college professor. When people started asking too many questions, he'd move on to another state or country.

At age 21, Abagnale was finally arrested. He served six months in a French prison, almost dying because of the terrible conditions. Eventually, he was brought to a U.S. prison. After his release, Abagnale started a company that teaches banks and law enforcement agencies to spot fraud.

7 Butch Cassidy

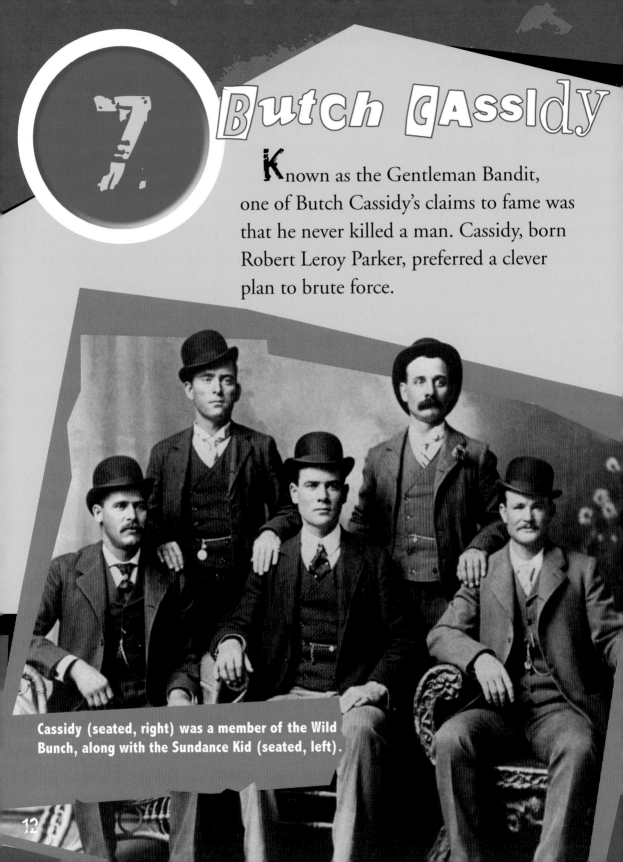

Known as the Gentleman Bandit, one of Butch Cassidy's claims to fame was that he never killed a man. Cassidy, born Robert Leroy Parker, preferred a clever plan to brute force.

Cassidy (seated, right) was a member of the Wild Bunch, along with the Sundance Kid (seated, left).

12

In 1894, Cassidy was in prison for bank robbery.

Cassidy joined a gang of robbers that police called the Wild Bunch. His closest friend in the gang was Harry Longabaugh, better known as the Sundance Kid. The gang robbed banks and trains throughout the West.

By 1901, the law was closing in on Cassidy and Longabaugh. They moved to Argentina, but U.S. detectives found out where they were. The pair then fled to Chile and Bolivia.

Cassidy's fate from there is uncertain. Reports say that in 1908, he and Longabaugh were cornered in a gunfight in Bolivia. Cassidy shot Longabaugh before taking his own life. Other stories say Cassidy returned to the United States and lived a clean life.

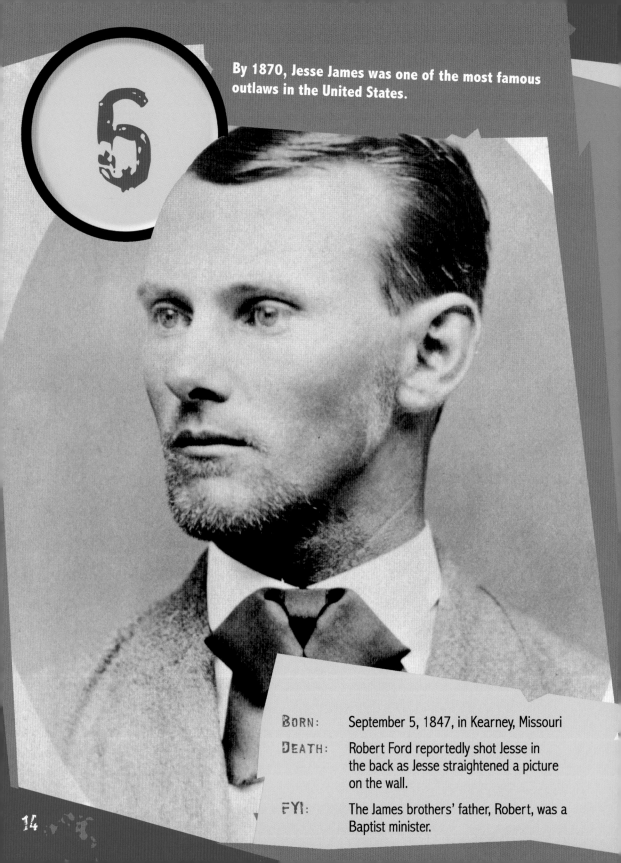

6

By 1870, Jesse James was one of the most famous outlaws in the United States.

BORN: September 5, 1847, in Kearney, Missouri

DEATH: Robert Ford reportedly shot Jesse in the back as Jesse straightened a picture on the wall.

FYI: The James brothers' father, Robert, was a Baptist minister.

JESSE JAMES

If you were in a bank or on a train in the late 1800s, Jesse James and his gang of outlaws were the last people you wanted to see.

James grew up in Missouri. At age 16, he fought on the Confederate side during the Civil War (1861–1865). After the war ended, he and his older brother, Frank, formed a gang with brothers Cole, Jim, and Bob Younger and several other men.

The James/Younger gang escaped capture for 10 years. On September 7, 1876, they rode into Northfield, Minnesota, and held up the bank. The townspeople armed themselves and put up a tremendous fight. Three gang members were killed, and the three Younger brothers were captured. Only the James brothers escaped.

A few years later, Jesse and Frank returned to Missouri and formed a new gang. In 1882, gang member Robert Ford killed Jesse to get the reward offered for his capture, dead or alive. After Jesse's death, Frank left crime behind, dying of natural causes in 1915.

In 1934, the FBI offered a $10,000 reward for Dillinger's capture, dead or alive.

JOHN HERBERT DILLINGER

On June 23, 1934, HOMER S. CUMMINGS, Attorney General of the United States, under the authority vested in him by an Act of Congress approved June 6, 1934, offered a reward of

$10,000.00

e capture of John Herbert D

reward of

John Dillinger

Few criminals had as rapid a rise and fall as John Dillinger. His career as a bank robber lasted just 14 months, but people still recognize his name.

Dillinger grew up in Indiana, joining a gang of troublemakers as a teenager. Following a botched armed robbery in 1924, Dillinger spent the next nine years in prison. After his release, he robbed several banks. He used the money to buy guns, which he smuggled to his former prison mates. They used the guns during a successful escape.

Dillinger and his gang robbed several banks throughout the Midwest during 1933 and early 1934. In 1934, Dillinger was arrested for the murder of a police officer. While in prison, he used a wooden gun to bluff his way out.

Dillinger quickly formed a new gang and went on the run. On July 22, 1934, FBI agents shot and killed him as he left a movie theater in Chicago.

BORN: June 22, 1903, in Indianapolis, Indiana

NICKNAME: Public Enemy Number One

FYI: About 5,000 people attended his funeral.

In 1933, Barrow and Parker stole cars and robbed businesses throughout the Midwest.

BORN: Parker—October 1, 1910, in Rowena, Texas; Barrow—March 21, 1909, in Telico, Texas

MOVIE: The 1967 movie *Bonnie and Clyde* brought new interest to their story.

FYI: Bonnie's poem "The Story of Bonnie and Clyde" was published in a newspaper after her death.

Bonnie And Clyde

When they were alive, Bonnie Parker and Clyde Barrow probably never imagined the reputation they would someday have. Their crime spree has become an American legend and the subject of books, TV shows, and movies.

In 1930, small-time criminal Clyde Barrow met 19-year-old waitress Bonnie Parker. The two fell in love, but soon after, Barrow was arrested and sent to prison. When Barrow was released, the couple started a series of violent robberies.

Their robberies, usually gas stations and grocery stores, seldom netted Barrow and Parker more than a few hundred dollars. But Barrow was ruthless when he was armed. He killed 12 people, including nine law enforcement officers.

By 1934, the law was closing in on the outlaw couple. On May 23, a group of officers ambushed their car in Louisiana. They peppered it with at least 100 bullets. Parker and Barrow were dead at the scene. Barrow was 25 years old, and Parker was just 23.

3

BORN: Sometime between 1859 and 1861, possibly in New York City

DIED: July 14, 1881

FYI: Legend says that Billy killed 21 men, but historians think it was about nine.

By 1880, Billy had spent three years on the run from the law.

Billy the Kid

To many, Billy the Kid is the most legendary outlaw of the Wild West. He is said to have began his criminal career at age 14.

Much of Billy's life is a mystery, including his birth date and real name. Some sources claim he was born Henry McCarty in 1859. Others say his name was William Bonney, born in 1861. As a boy, Billy moved with his family to Kansas, Colorado, and New Mexico. There, he was jailed for stealing clothes from a laundry. After two days, he escaped.

After killing a man in Arizona in 1877, Billy was constantly on the run. He ended up back in New Mexico, working as a ranch hand. In 1878, Billy's boss, John Tunstall, stood up to a group of ranchers who were trying to take his land. Tunstall was killed. Billy hunted down and killed several of the men who had killed Tunstall—including a sheriff.

In April 1881, Sheriff Pat Garrett caught Billy. Billy was found guilty of murder. He then escaped from jail by killing a guard and a deputy. Garrett tracked Billy throughout the Southwest until he shot and killed him three months later.

2

In May 1929, Philadelphia police officers arrested Capone for carrying a concealed weapon. He served nine months in jail.

0725

S 16 29

AL CAPONE

Al Capone has been dead for about 60 years, but most people still know his name. Born in Brooklyn, New York, Capone belonged to teenage gangs in the city. In 1920, the 20th Amendment to the U.S. Constitution outlawed the manufacture, sale, and transportation of alcoholic products. Criminals who broke this law were called bootleggers. At age 21, Capone moved to Chicago and got into the bootlegging business.

By 1925, Capone was on his way to becoming the most famous and powerful gangster in the world. He was credited with ordering the murders of at least 200 people, including police officers and other gangsters. But his criminal career ended because of a much less violent crime.

In 1931, Capone was convicted of not paying his taxes. He was one of the first convicts to enter the famous prison on Alcatraz Island in 1934. Released in 1939, Capone died in 1947 at age 48.

BORN: January 17, 1899, in Brooklyn, New York

NICKNAME: Scarface, but his associates called
            him Snorky

FYI: On February 14, 1929, Capone ordered an
            ambush. The "St. Valentine's Day Massacre"
            killed seven gangsters.

Gotti's wardrobe of expensive suits earned him the nickname "Dapper Don."

BORN: October 27, 1940, in the Bronx, New York

EDUCATION: Expelled from the eighth grade and never returned to school

FYI: In 2004, Gotti's daughter and grandsons starred in a reality TV series called *Growing Up Gotti*.

John Gotti

John Gotti was the most famous gangster since Al Capone. During the 1980s, he attracted reporters, photographers, and TV cameras wherever he went.

Gotti was a member of the Gambino crime family in New York City. In 1985, he took over its leadership by plotting the murder of the family's boss on a New York City street.

Gotti was tried for a number of crimes, including murder, selling illegal drugs, and assault. But he avoided convictions by bribing jurors and scaring witnesses. This gave him the nickname "Teflon Don," because law enforcement officers couldn't make any of the charges stick.

Gotti's reign ended in 1992 when one of his associates, Sammy "The Bull" Gravano, testified against him. Gotti was convicted and spent the last 10 years of his life in prison. He died of cancer in 2002.

The World's Most Notorious Crooks

10

Victor Lustig

9

Willie Sutton

8

Frank Abagnale

7

Butch Cassidy

Jesse James

6

5

John Dillinger

4

Bonnie and Clyde

3

Billy the Kid

2

Al Capone

John Gotti

1

understanding criminals

People love to talk and learn about famous criminals and their crimes. Their daring plans and narrow escapes make fascinating legends. Books, movies, and songs are great ways to tell their stories.

But despite all the attention they received, these criminals didn't lead glamorous lives. Many of them turned to crime because they thought they had few other choices. Most died or spent years in prison because of their decisions. Sure, they lived exciting lives for a time. But in the end, their crimes cost them far more than they gained. They proved that crime really doesn't pay.

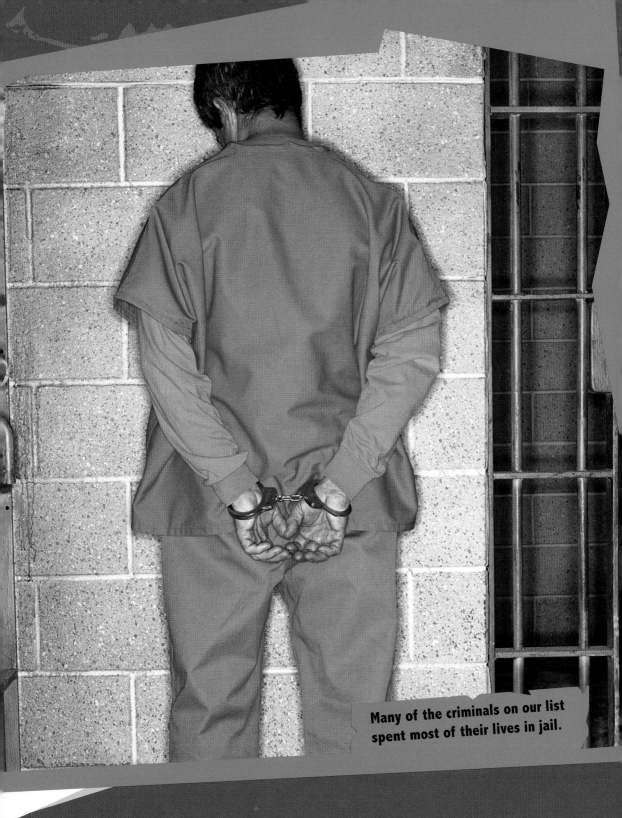

Many of the criminals on our list
spent most of their lives in jail.

GLOSSARY

alias (AY-lee-uhss)—a false name, especially one used by a criminal

ambush (AM-bush)—a surprise attack

bootleg (BOOT-leg)—to illegally make, transport, or sell alcohol

con artist (KON AR-tist)—a person who uses false promises to get the money or possessions of others

counterfeit (KOUN-tur-fit)—something fake that looks like the real thing, such as counterfeit money

disguise (diss-GIZE)—a costume that hides who a person is

fraud (FRAWD)—a person or thing that is not what it seems or is represented to be

heist (HIEST)—an armed robbery

READ MORE

Landau, Elaine. *Jesse James: Wild West Train Robber.* Best of the West Biographies. Berkeley Heights, N.J.: Enslow, 2004.

Thomas, Paul. *Outlaws.* History Makers. North Mankato, Minn.: Smart Apple Media, 2002.

Townsend, John. *Organized Crime.* True Crime. Chicago: Raintree, 2005.

Yancey, Diane. *Al Capone.* Heroes and Villains. San Diego: Lucent, 2003.

INTERNET SITES

FactHound offers a safe, fun way to find Internet sites related to this book. All of the sites on FactHound have been researched by our staff.

Here's how:

1. Visit *www.facthound.com*
2. Choose your grade level.
3. Type in this book ID **0736864407** for age-appropriate sites. You may also browse subjects by clicking on letters, or by clicking on pictures and words.
4. Click on the **Fetch It** button.

FactHound will fetch the best sites for you!

INDEX